# Contents

# Safety

## It's never too early to teach your child the importance of keeping safe.

Make sure that your child is aware of everyday dangers, but do not trust him/her to always remember.

- Keep hot and sharp things out of reach.

- Use plastic beakers, not glass.

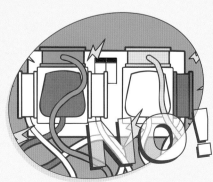

- Do not overload electrical sockets.

# Safety

● Check smoke alarms regularly.

● Keep all medicines in childproof containers in a locked cupboard.

● Do not let children see you taking tablets.

● Do not use electrical appliances in the bathroom.

● Keep all cleaning products and chemicals out of reach and in their original containers.

# Safety

● Do not let your child breathe smoke.

● Second-hand smoke can lead to heart disease and lung cancer and can make illnesses like asthma worse.

● Keep your whole house smoke free.

● If you are a smoker why not quit and enjoy better health and more money for you and your family.

Contact your GP or Health Visitor for advice on how to quit, or ring the No Smoking Quitline on

## 0800 00 22 00

## OUT & ABOUT

- Do not let your child play in the street.

Remember, always **stop**, **look** and **listen** before crossing the road.

- Teach your child how to cross the road safely with you.

- Find safe places to cross the road.

- Wear bright colours at night to be seen.

- Always hold hands when you are near the road.

- Make sure that your child always travels in a child's car seat, ideally in the back of a car, for ALL journeys however short.

# Healthy Eating

- A varied and balanced diet is important for all the family.

Lots of fruit and vegetables - at least 5 portions every day

Some fish, meat or alternatives

Some milk and dairy products

Plenty of bread, cereal, rice, pasta or potatoes

Try to restrict fatty and sugary foods

...and plenty of water!

- Give your child a variety of different foods to help ensure that he/she gets all the different vitamins and minerals that are needed for healthy growth.

# Healthy Eating

● Don't give up on foods that your child doesn't like. Try them again at a later date or prepared in a different way.

● If your child doesn't like cooked vegetables try blending them into soups, casseroles and sauces, or give raw vegetables instead.

● Encourage your child to eat a 'rainbow of fruit and vegetables' every day (five different colours).

# Healthy Eating

● Do not allow your child to fill up on snacks or fizzy drinks in between meals.

● Children love to copy, so the best way to encourage good eating habits is to sit down and eat together at the table.

● Eating three times a day with a small snack mid-morning and one mid-afternoon is a good pattern to follow for most children.

# Healthy Eating

Take care with food hygiene to keep your family healthy.

- Make sure that everyone washes their hands before eating or preparing food and always after visiting the toilet.

- Store chilled foods correctly.

- Make sure that all food is cooked thoroughly.

- If reheating food, always ensure that it is piping hot. Do not reheat food more than once.

- Clean kitchen surfaces thoroughly, especially after handling raw meat.

- Wash dishcloths and empty bins daily.

# Oral Hygiene

Teach your child how to brush his/her teeth:

- Use a small, pea size blob of fluoride toothpaste.

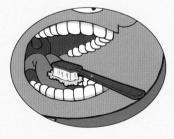

- Brush at the front.

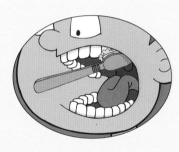

- Brush at the back.

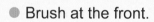

- Brush on top of the teeth.

- Brush behind the teeth.

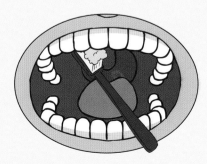

# Oral Hygiene

● Spit out the toothpaste.

● Rinse the brush.

● Let Mum or Dad have a turn.

● Brush for two minutes.

● Make sure that you follow this routine with your child every morning and every night before bed.

# Oral Hygiene

Sweets and sugary drinks are best kept for special treats, preferably straight after meals, when they do least damage to the teeth.

Fruit, raw vegetables, bread and natural yogurt make good snacks between meals.

Water or milk is the best between-meal drink.

# Oral Hygiene

Plain crisps are not bad for teeth, but they do contain fat and salt, which should only be eaten in small amounts. Many flavoured crisps also contain sugar, which is bad for teeth.

Low-sugar or diet drinks contain artificial sweeteners. Do not give too many drinks containing the artificial sweetener saccharin.

The sugar in dried fruit and fruit juice can cause tooth decay if consumed frequently, so keep them for mealtimes.

# Keeping Active

Keeping active is good for all the family. Everybody should aim for 30 minutes of exercise every day.

- Walk instead of using the bus or car.

- Enjoy your local pool.

Many pools have special water confidence sessions for under fives.

# Keeping Active

● Join a class.

● Ride a bike.

● Don't forget high factor sun cream and sun hats when the sun is shining.

# Keeping Active

● Enjoy games.

● Play ball.

● Visit the park.

# Keeping Active

Take the stairs instead of the lift.

Exercise by getting the jobs done.

# Early Learning

Children learn by example and love to copy their parents.
You are your child's greatest teacher.

- If you are loving and caring, your child will learn to be loving and caring.

Happy Birthday Mummy!

It's ok darling, it's only a graze. We'll soon make you better.

- If you are calm, your child will learn to be calm.

... and I catched a fish that was this big!

- If you listen, your child will learn to listen.

# Early Learning

- If you talk to your child, your child will learn to talk.

- If you praise your child, your child will feel valued.

- If you have time for your child, your child will have time for you.

# Early Learning

- Listen carefully and give your child the chance to finish talking.

- Take turns to speak.

- Talk to your child about things that are happening around you.

- Repetition is an important part of learning. Be prepared to repeat new words and phrases many times.

# Early Learning

Play group is a great place to help your child learn how to mix with other children and try lots of new activities.

This is fun, Mummy

Encourage your child to put toys away as part of the game.

# Early Learning

Encourage your child to be independent.

# Early Learning

- Share books. Talking about the pictures or the stories is a great way to help your child to develop language skills and understanding.

- Reading bedtime stories is a wonderful, calming way to end the day.

- Visit your local library to find great books for all the family. Many libraries also have special story-time sessions for their young visitors.

- Always praise your child for good behaviour.

- If your child misbehaves always explain what he/she has done wrong and why it is wrong.

- **NEVER HIT YOUR CHILD.**

# Contacts

In case of an accident, emergency or just advice these are some useful numbers to ring for information and help.

## NHS Direct 0845 4647 (England & Wales)

Your call will automatically be put through to your nearest centre and will be charged at local rates (may be more from a mobile).

www.nhsdirect.nhs.uk        www.nhsdirect.wales.nhs.uk

## NHS24 (Scotland) 08454 24 24 24 www.nhs24.com

Your local Health Visitor can be contacted via your GP practice.

Add your GP's number here

**Your local Fire Service** can be contacted for advice on fire prevention.

**Child Accident Prevention Trust (CAPT) 020 7608 3828**
A charity committed to reducing childhood injury.
www.capt.org.uk

**Royal Society for the Prevention of Accidents (RoSPA)**
**0121 248 2000**
www.rospa.com

**Useful numbers in your area:**

# Three
# is a Magic Number

is the fifth book in the series

## Caring for Kids

Also available:

## DON'T FORGET:

All children develop at different rates. The ages here are only a guide to your child's development. However, if you are concerned about your child's development, help and advice are always available.

A list of useful telephone numbers of people who are happy to help can be found on the left.

Also available from Kid Premiership Early Years:

www.**kidpremiershi**p.com

# Caring for Kids - Book 5

As your child develops and grows there are many new things that you will experience.

**THREE IS A MAGIC NUMBER** is packed with essential information for you and your 3 year old on:

## Safety

## Keeping Active

## Healthy Eating

## Early Learning

## Oral Hygiene

**THREE IS A MAGIC NUMBER** is the fifth book in the series **CARING FOR KIDS.** Also available:

ISBN 978-1-906036-08-9

www.**kidpremiership**.com

📞 01484 668008  📘 01484 668009  ✉ mail@kidpremiership.cc

One17ED, The Dyehouse, Armitage Bridge, Huddersfield, HD4 7F

# Woodworker Manual of Finishing and Polishing 2nd Edition

## Charles D. Cliffe

## ARGUS BOOKS